Perspective

Smrutiprava Dash

Presentation by *BookLeaf Publishing*

Web: www.bookleafpub.com

E-mail: info@bookleafpub.com

ISBN: 9789360940720

First edition 2024

To all those who seek to find strength in their struggles and light in their darkest moments, this book is for you.

ACKNOWLEDGEMENT

Creating this collection of poems has been a journey of introspection, discovery, and transformation, and I am deeply grateful to those who have supported me along the way.
First and foremost, I wish to thank my family for their unwavering belief in my passion for poetry. Your love and encouragement have been the cornerstone of my creative endeavors, providing me with the strength and inspiration to pursue my dreams.

To my friends, who have been my sounding boards and critics, your honest feedback and endless support have helped shape these poems into their best possible versions. Your insights have been invaluable, and your companionship has made this journey all the more meaningful.
A special thanks to my mentors and teachers, who have nurtured my love for literature and the written word. Your guidance has been instrumental in my growth as a poet, and your wisdom continues to inspire me.

To my readers, who have found solace, joy, or reflection in my words, I am deeply humbled and grateful. Your connection with my poetry is the ultimate reward for my efforts, and I hope these verses have resonated with you in a way that enriches your own perspectives.

Lastly, to the muses of everyday life, the moments of beauty, struggle, love, and loss that sparked the verses within these pages, thank you for being the wellspring of my creativity. It is through these experiences that I have learned to see the world through an elastic lens, and I am honored to share that vision with you.

With heartfelt gratitude,

Smrutiprava Dash

PREFACE

Embracing the Strength in Perspective

In the intricate tapestry of human experience, perspective is the thread that weaves together our understanding of the world. It is the lens through which we interpret joy and sorrow, triumph and defeat. Yet, too often, our perspectives become rigid, like a tightly knotted rope, constricting our potential and deepening our wounds. This preface is an invitation to reimagine perspective not as a source of limitation but as a boundless, elastic force that can adapt, transform, and ultimately strengthen us.

Consider the rope: a single knot might tighten with strain, but what if our perspectives were more like elastic bands? Elasticity allows for resilience and flexibility. When stretched, it does not break; it adjusts, returns to form, and retains its essence. This is the kind of perspective we must cultivate, one that acknowledges pain but also seeks growth, one that finds light in the shadows.

Every moment of sadness or disappointment can be a seed for newfound strength and understanding. It is through the elasticity of our perspectives that we can embrace challenges as opportunities and sorrows as lessons. This transformative outlook does not diminish our experiences; rather, it enriches them, imbuing our lives with a deeper sense of purpose and resilience.

Let this be a guide for those moments when the weight of the world feels too heavy. Let it remind us that within each of us lies the power to reshape our narratives. By adopting an elastic perspective, we can face adversity with grace and emerge stronger, more compassionate, and profoundly human.

In these pages, you will find not just poems and reflections, but a call to action to stretch your mind, to bend without breaking, and to find strength in the very flexibility of your outlook. May this preface serve as a beacon, guiding you towards a perspective that empowers and uplifts, no matter the circumstances.

Smrutiprava Dash

My words are not mere words;
They are reflections of your feelings.
I don't ask you to follow my instructions;
I ask you to listen to yourself.
My aim is to help you become empty
So that your emptiness can embrace peace.
I'm here to remind you who you are.

Your dream is to be
A breeze encircling the bare trees,
A wildflower with an urge to smile,
A bird that sings without approval,
A sea that loves its waves,
And nature that nurtures.

Have you ever been left
By roommates, friends, lovers,
Or anyone who once found hope in you?
Have you ever been homeless?
You've experienced all the worst possible for
you,
But even in the darkness, there was still you
For introspection,
For motivation to feel alive.
Don't be disheartened;
No matter what, you will find
What you need, if not what you want.

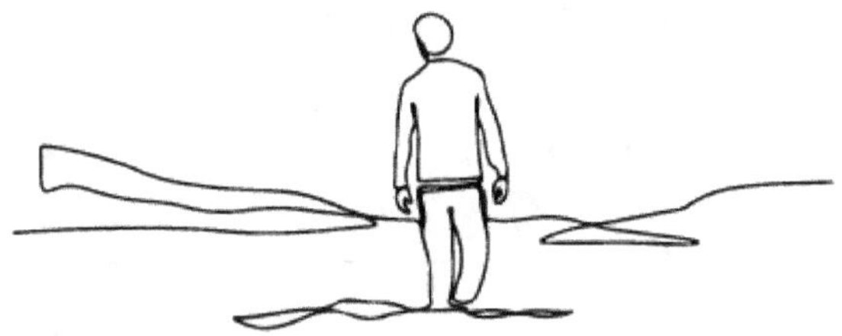

Regardless of the situation,
No matter what you feel
Scattered, strong, or so-called strong
Allow yourself to feel.
Anything that comes your way,
Remember, only humans make errors
And learn to become wise.
Don't search for the right way;
Acknowledge that you are on the right path.

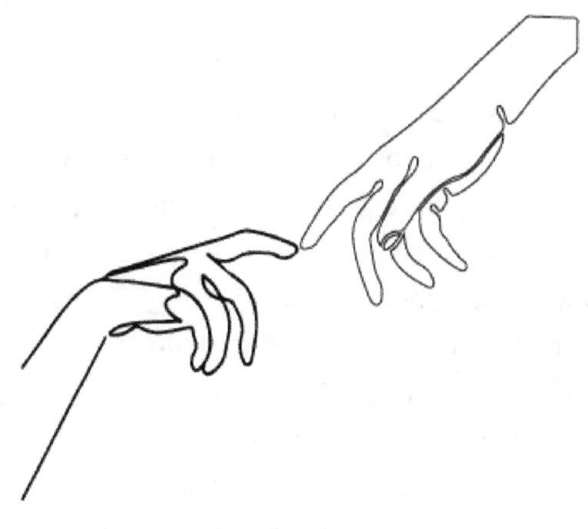

It wasn't easy
To believe someone, but you did.
Then it was harder
To trust after being cheated.
Still, you believed.
They called you a loser,
But you knew you were brave.
As it takes courage to trust someone
After being betrayed.

It took you years to understand
That music videos are just scripted reality,
And movies are examples of an ideal life
That it's not essential to have a desire for it.
What if they don't even exist?
Everything you love and find interesting
May not be real.
Not all that glitters is gold.
When you broke free from that trap,
You discovered the power of being real.
The more authentic you became,
The more you found people to be genuine.

You are a lost child now,
Innocence traded for boldness.
But who said boldness means acting?
You can be real, like a child
That is true boldness.
You've lost your transparency
As the world demands you play a part.

You became "mature,"
Yet true maturity is being transparent
While understanding others' feelings.
You lost true love,
Afraid to let your heartbreak.
Didn't you cry freely as a child?
Didn't you laugh with your whole heart?
Who told you to give up your childishness?
Accept yourself as you are.

Don't fall into the trap
Of marks, money, and status.
When you can celebrate life with nothing,
Only then will you have everything.

Love is not easy.
It's not merely about someone's body,
Not emotional dependency,
Nor psychological needs.
Love is not simply loving
Because someone loves your back.
True love is seeing them at their worst,
Yet loving them at their best.
It's accepting their individuality,
And wanting them to grow and heal.
Love has the power to let go,
To let live, to let be.
And even after letting go,
It still remains love.

It's not love; the world is blind.
Everyone is in a race
A race for money, status, luxury.
No one loves themselves.
Not husbands, not wives,
Not parents, not even nature.
They all want to be someone.
But who told you that you aren't enough?
Who told you to chase perfection?
It's not society,
Not your neighbors.
It's your own insecurity,
Your belief that you are insufficient.

You compare,
You compete,
And in that race,
You lose yourself.
You keep running,
For the rest of your life.
But the truth is,
Everything you want,
You already have.
You just don't love it.

Unhappiness is healthy,
Yet you believe it's a curse.
Happiness is bliss
But can you truly taste happiness
Without ever feeling the discomfort of pain?
Isn't it pain that makes you appreciate pleasure?
A bad friend that reveals the good ones?
If life were only happiness,
Only pleasure and all things good,
Would you even enjoy it,
Without knowing its opposite?
So why do you blame yourself
For not being happy?
Accept every flavor life gives you.
Only then will you discover
The best recipe.

You want to be good, only good
In the eyes of others,
Shaped by their opinions.
You seek validation outside yourself,
Believing in astrology
Because you don't believe in you.
You trust others' words
Because you don't truly know yourself.

You hide your flaws,
Your habits,
Your behavior
Unwilling to accept who you are.
You fear being real,
Afraid of being hated.

But you can be good to yourself
And to others
Without compromise.
It happens when you find clarity,
When you sit with your thoughts
And understand
What hurts you,
What makes you happy.
When you gain that understanding,
You're no longer a puppet
To others' opinions.

What you have
Stuff, ideas, people,
A multitude of tasks.
You are burdened by it all.

The one who has much
Cannot care for one thing properly.
So, hold onto yourself and your essentials.
Choose yourself first,
Then choose what belongs to you.

Tend to the small things with ease
And keep doing so.
Let go of the unnecessary.
Allow those who wish to leave, to depart.
Consume only what your body needs.
Be minimal and be your best.
The more organized you are,
The more your life will flourish.

You think success lies
In a big house, expensive cars,
Luxurious comforts.
You chase these,
Yet if you're unhappy now,
You'll remain unhappy with more.
You'll only crave endlessly,
Always filling a void.

True success is love
To give love and be reciprocated,
Even by an animal or a book.
Anything or anyone that you can love,
Or who can love you.

True success is finding yourself.
And when you find yourself,
You find your God.
You see that God in everything,
And your success
Transforms into happiness.

The key to confidence
Doesn't lie in the clothes you wear,
The brand you carry,
Or even your physical form.

It's the clarity of who you are
The acceptance of yourself,
Knowing that what you are
Is your best.

If you think
Everyone loves you as you are
You radiate confidence.

You do yoga,
You meditate,
Engage in charity,
Pursue great deeds.
Yet fulfillment remains elusive
If you lack clarity
About what you're doing
And who you are.

It's crucial to know your purpose,
Not merely to copy others,
Thinking their actions
Will bring you success.
Do what is yours to do.
Know yourself deeply,
And have clarity of purpose
Understand why you are doing this.

A king may rise to his throne through destiny,
but fate alone cannot make him a good king.
He could be cruel, brutal, and evil, or
he could choose to be peace-loving and serve his
people.
It is his choices that define him, not fate.

Fate may grant power or position,
but even an ordinary person
can be regarded as a king
for their noble qualities.
In the end, it is one's actions that
earn the love and respect
befitting a true ruler,
not the hand of destiny.

People fight with one another
When they have no energy left
To battle within themselves.

In times of adversity,
Even those closest to us
Turn against each other.

Staying in one place,
Repeating the same actions,
Is not called experience;
It's called being trapped.

To go beyond your current experience
Is to heal.
It's like tasting something sour,
Knowing it's sour,
Yet continuing to taste it
In hopes of making it normal.

Instead, understand what you need.
Perhaps sugar,
Or something else entirely,
Might be the right fit for you.

Who told you that one is one,
Two is two,
A cow is a cow,
And a cat is a cat?
See things as they are.
Universal truths are accepted universally,
So, they are universal.

You've forgotten that you are the universe,
That you interpret things in your own manner.
You've silenced that perspective.
You are troubled by triggers
Stored from the past,
Not by the present situation.

It's like having the flu within you,
So, you become sensitive
Even to something as simple as water.
You are all in a trap.
You think you are free,
But you are merely repeating past incidents,
Clinging to your philosophies,
Making assumptions and hypotheses.
These are your sources of suffering.
Those who are trapped are suffering,
While those who are truly free
Are celebrating.

You guard yourself from the sharpness of love's
embrace,
As well as from the cold void of its absence.
Let neither the fervor of affection
Nor the silence of solitude pierce your heart.
In the space between these extremes,
May you find solace,
Neither too touched nor too untouched,
But steady in the quiet expanse of your own
being.

You are born free,
Yet you're taught to believe
Everything you were told.
Morality often robs you
Of the right to question
And see beyond explanations.
What would you be
If you were told
You are free
And your life is in your own hands?

You must learn the art of sadness,
The act of aggression,
And the depths of misery,
So that you can find happiness,
Attain peace,
And create your own life.

It's free,
All the money,
Name and fame,
Good jobs and bad experiences.
what is truly expensive
Is liberty from money,
Freedom from name and fame.
It's a luxury
To know oneself.

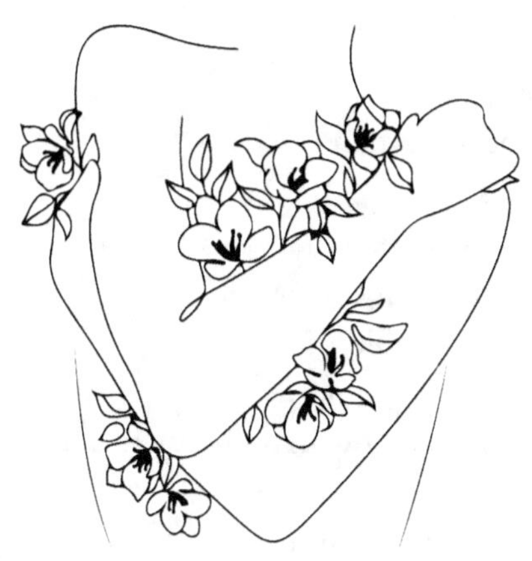

If you don't know
How to love yourself,
How can you love others?
If you don't make your bed,
Why would you make bed for others?
If you can't make yourself good food,
How can you cook for others?

What you see around
Is a circus,
And you are entertained.
When you become a part of it,
You feel miserable,
Constantly being told
What to do and how to do it
Without asking why.
Is it any less than a circus,
Your life?

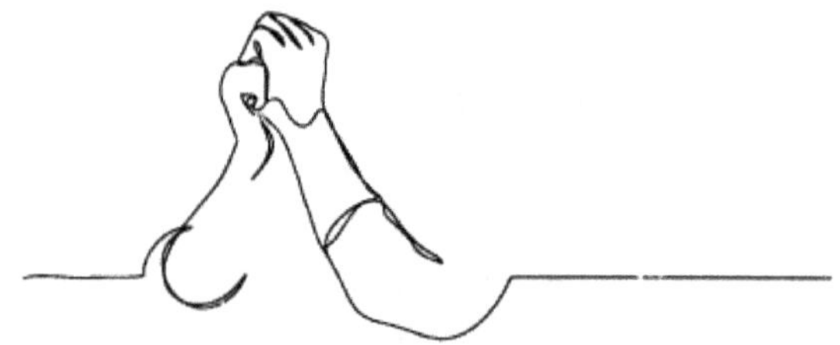

You lost someone dear to you,
Who will not come back.
But you live more for him,
For he lives in you.
You are not apart,
Even if he is not with you.
He is always driving your intentions,
He is your inspiration.
So, he lives more and dies less.
Death never leaves us apart
It's our memories
That never gets recreated
So we feel a part of us is lost.

You love to sit in nature,
Not to escape your daily schedule,
But to be nature itself.
To be the stream of water,
And the wind in the air,
To be wild and free.
To tolerate all,
And explode when it's too much.

You used to think that
A good man is one
Whose intentions are good.
But you realized that
A good man is someone
Who has the capacity to be bad,
Yet with all his strength,
Chooses to be good.
An inexperienced person
Cannot be truly good or bad;
Only an experienced person
Can be trusted based on
The choices they make.

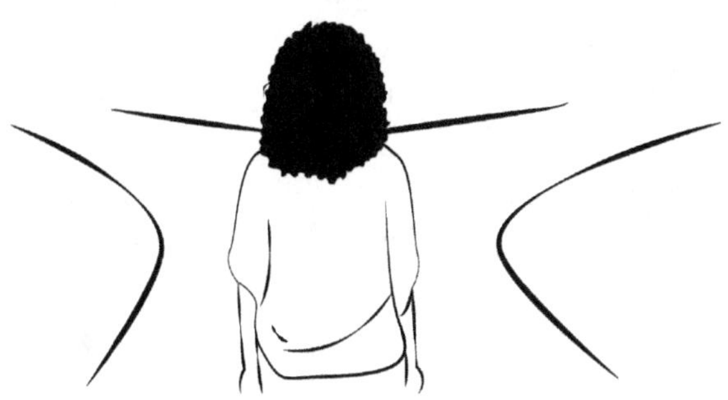

A great mind always suffers,
For few can truly understand it,
And it can connect with only a select few.
Yet, it enjoys life,
Being well aware of the truth.
Even as it breathes,
It draws in only fresh air,
Unaffected by pollution.

What will remain after you?
Your voice, your contributions,
Your smile and your aliveness
Not your money and power
Which is the source for existence
Don't make that source of existence.

When some things appear good,
others will seem bad
it's all a matter of situation and timing.
What brings peace today
might bring conflict tomorrow.
There's no absolute power in external things to
move you;
it's your internal perspective that interprets them
as good or bad,
easy or hard.
There are no fixed rules
it's all in how you perceive it.

It's you who acts without acting,
who gives without expecting.
You don't get hurt when
you don't rely on others' perspectives,
because you know you're doing it
not to be seen,
but because it needs to be done.
You let go of the outcome,
allowing your actions to
last forever as a true reflection of yourself.

If you admire the rich,
the poor may feel neglected.
If you focus on having more,
insecurity spreads across the world.
So instead, you accept yourself
as the best version of you
without possessions, without a name.
Who you are is what you build,
and that is what makes you human,
beyond the rat race, at peace, in true freedom.
This is your only true desire,
though you may have forgotten it.

Water is the most essential element;
it cleanses and sustains life.
Yet, it remains close to the ground.
Even when it falls from the sky,
it descends to embrace the earth,
becoming accessible to all.
It serves many, relying on none.
Like water, stay grounded to reach all, cleanse
all, and serve all
while remaining clear, pure, and essential.

Whenever you strive for perfection,
you'll always feel a little less.
No matter how much you improve,
there will always be someone better.
So don't try too hard to be the best
you'll become a prisoner of others' opinions.
Instead, do what you love
with full awareness and purpose.
Relax, and everything will be alright.

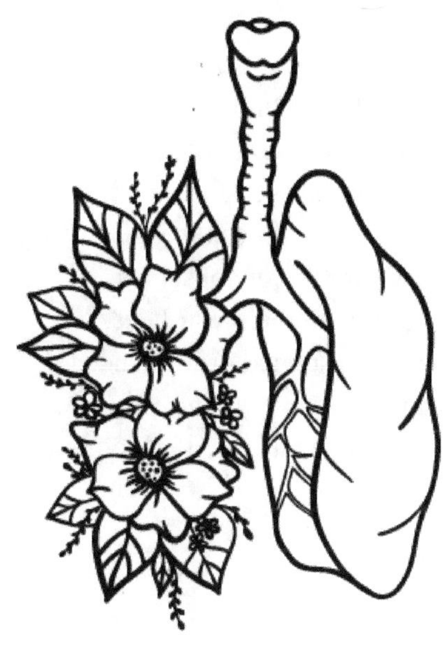

A house is made of walls,
and we do our best to create beautiful walls and
a sturdy roof.
Yet, it's the emptiness inside that we use and
value.
No matter how strong a vessel is,
it's the empty space within that holds water.
So, it's not just what you become that gives you
worth
it's the emptiness within that always guides you.

Too much light can blind,
too much color can confuse,
too much love can spoil,
and too much thought can weaken the mind.
So, the observer merely observes,
seeing things with the inward eye,
not to be overwhelmed or influenced,
but to understand everything
while remaining unaffected by coming and
going.

Climb to the top of the tree,
and your feet will be shaky.
Jump, and you risk breaking a leg or a hand.
Stay on the ground, and you'll remain balanced.
Success is precarious
it's dangerous to rise above all,
carrying the constant fear of falling.
True success is finding peace,
no matter where you are.

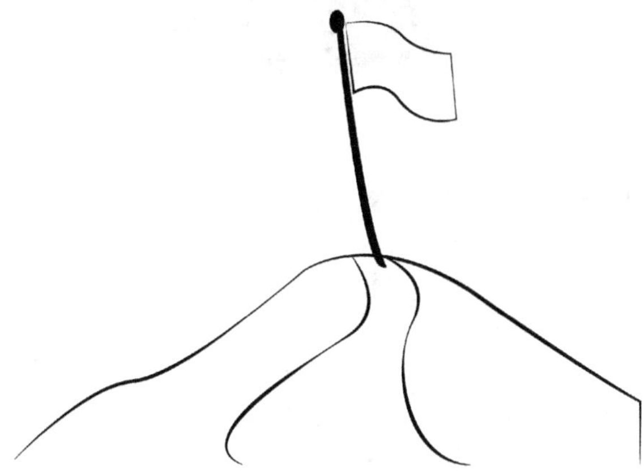

The essence of all wisdom is you;
it cannot be removed.
It cannot be seen or heard,
touched or untouched.
It is your own soul,
where you have come from
neither the beginning nor the end,
but both nothing and everything at the same
time.

Morality is often the cause of suffering,
laws the reason for misdeeds,
and justice the source of dissatisfaction.
Profit and loss are the reasons for theft and
cheating.

Let go of what man has created,
and disregard what others claim God wants from
you.
Did they truly converse with God?
If God sees all, wouldn't He communicate
directly?
Instead, seek answers from your own
intelligence
your soul knows the truth better than anything
else.

You're free from the attachment to the wisdom
of right and wrong.
You choose to be foolish when you could call
yourself wise.
You dwell in darkness and do not seek the light.
You are homeless because four walls cannot
contain the wind.
You are not wealthy, but you are nature itself,
The source of existence.
You have nothing material,
Yet you are full of life, like the wind, rain, and
sand.

Be a part if you want to be whole.
Be lost if you want to be found.
Give if you want to receive.
People are remembered because they remember.
People are worshipped because they worship.
They are listened to because they listen.
When someone doesn't seek the spotlight,
they become a beacon.
When they don't demand, they receive
everything.
When they have nothing to prove, people trust
their words.
With no goal in mind, they win every game.

Those who seem powerful to others
often lack the ability to empower themselves.
Standing tall often means straining on tiptoe.
Those who rush seldom reach far.
If you constantly explain yourself,
it shows you don't truly know who you are.
Clinging to everything leaves you with nothing.
Simply do your work and let go.

Whoever bears a name on this earth
Possesses something uniquely their own
Their own words, their own theories,
Or their own way of doing things.
Those who learn much from others
Often know little about themselves.
So, you must ask yourself:
What are you beyond imitation?
Will you embrace someone
Who is busy creating their own path?
Or will you command them to follow another's
lead?

Stay constant, stay consistent.
All places belong to your mind,
but your heart is home.
What is the point of wandering
if your mind can't find peace?
What role does a home serve?
If it fills you with thoughts that lead to restless
nights?
If you are always on the move,
you'll lose touch with yourself.
Yet, to be distracted and disturbed
Is to learn how not to be.
Return to the basics
Your heaviness will find light within you,
And in your stillness,
you will discover true movement.

A man is not solely masculine,
And a woman is not solely feminine.
Both qualities reside in each of us.
Don't discard the feminine—embrace the
masculine.
Don't disrespect the masculine—accept the
feminine.
Both are integral to the fabric of nature.
Black and white are essential;
Without black, there is no white.
They define each other,
Each with its own unique aspects.
All opposites are necessary;
Don't discard one and embrace the other.
Life's perfection lies in balance,
And your own perfection requires you to accept
the world as it is.
It's selfish to love only what you need
And hate what you don't.
Everything has its place in time,
So don't despise someone simply because they
are different from you.

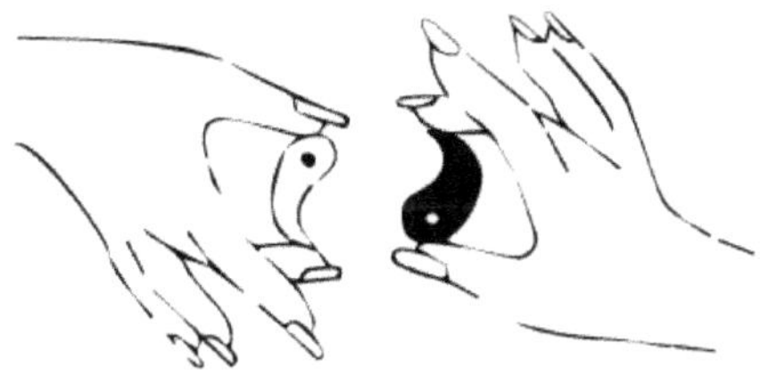

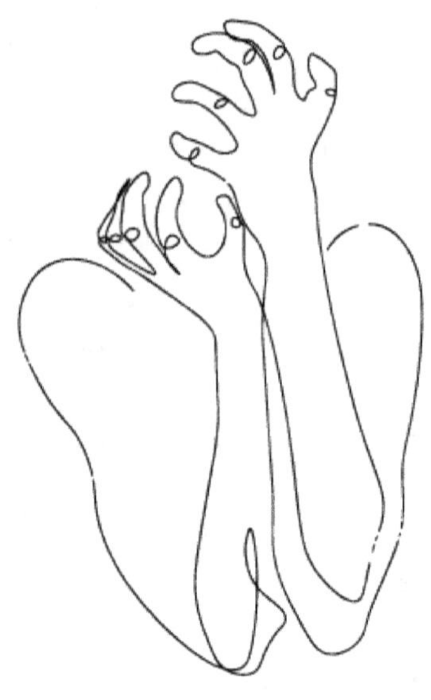

Definitions are man-made,
And whatever is made by man
Creates conflict,
As each person's choices differ.
Without distinctions,
Without names for things,
The world is just a void
Nothing more.

Do not try to control the world or force change.
The world doesn't need to be altered, improved,
Modified, or advanced.
It doesn't demand performance.
Instead, the world asks for your patience
To give yourself time,
To take some rest,
And to do the things that make you feel safe.
You're encouraged by the world to prioritize
your well-being.
Nothing ever changed by being controlled
but with patience, so let it be.

If you feel the need to prove your point, you lose
your calm.
What is the value of winning if success doesn't
bring you peace?
Those who possess clarity don't need to prove
themselves;
They understand that true clarity is found within,
not through external validation.
The truly wealthy are those who give, not those
who take.
A taker is driven by ego and power,
While a giver finds peace in their generosity.
Don't seek to control—lead instead.
Don't hold possessions for yourself,
But share them with others.

What is the point of electrical advancements
If humanity remains in the darkness of
ignorance?
What is the value of technological progress
If people become cheap and nature is priced
beyond reach?
True contentment would be possible
If the world were governed by wise and caring
hands.
No one would need to escape
If they found peace within their own home.
No one would gossip about others
If they focused on being a helping hand.
What is the purpose of what the government
does
When people are becoming slaves to their own
ignorance?

If you are truly peaceful,
You respond without words,
Help without being asked,
And conquer without strategy.
You love the entire universe
As if it were your own home,
And accept everything just as it is.

Knowledge is an illusion.
No matter how much you know,
You will always know less.
True wisdom lies in embracing the unknown.
Having nothing is true wealth,
And appearing foolish is a sign of insight.
Only when you are injured
Do you seek medicine?
Only when you become nothing
Can you become everything?

Who is truly the best?
The one who wishes for others to be their best.
Only the insecure seek to undermine others.
One who knows everything
Is always ready to listen to others.
A person skilled in profit and loss
Serves the well-being of others.
The best leader understands others,
And the true philosopher
Bows before a child,
For this is what makes them truly great.

Have no desires,
and you will have nothing to lose.
Have no possessions,
and you will have nothing to fear.
Have nothing,
and you will be liberated.

If change is the only constant,
Why cling to the unchanging?
If you are uncertain about the future,
Why worry excessively?
If you can simply eat, sleep, and help those in
need,
What is the point of competition and
comparison?

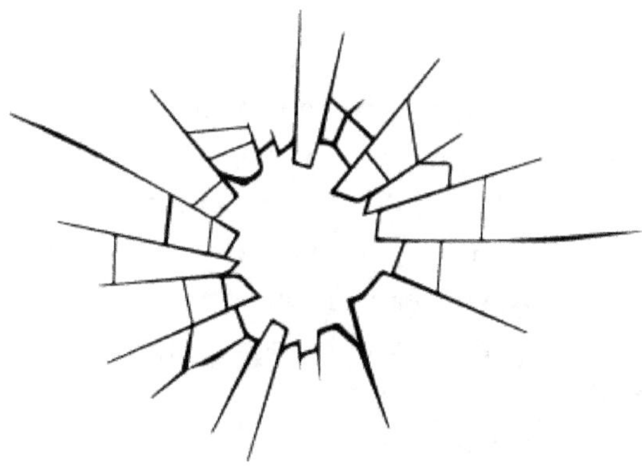

If your mindset is rigid,
You will suffer.
If you are inflexible,
You will find no comfort, even in your comfort
zone.
Those who are gentle endure longer,
While those who are hard break both others and
themselves.

Mistakes are part of being human.
When you make them, admit them,
correct them, and strive not to repeat them.
Again, you make new mistakes
In this way, you learn and grow.
Even in old age, a wise person continues to learn.
Those who stop learning, believing they know enough,
Are the ones who become rigid, stiff, and stagnant.

Fear is the greatest illusion,
stripping away the essence of truly living.
The deepest misery lies in being disturbed by an
enemy,
but if you are free from fear, you are truly safe.

Words that are hard to remember are not wise.
It's the simple words that leave a lasting trace in
the mind.
A truly wise man remains in people's hearts,
not for his words, but for his actions.
It's not the person who constantly speaks
words of wisdom who is truly intellectual.
True intelligence often resides in silence.
Similarly, art that is complex is not necessarily
great art.
The greatest art is that which feels alive and has
a purpose
art that speaks to the soul.

If you rely on others to bring you happiness,
you will never be truly happy.
Happiness comes from within.
If you seek money to feel complete,
money will only make you crave more.
Be content with what you have;
happiness cannot be found in wanting more.
Desire has no end.
The sole method to free yourself from
it is to cherish what you already have.

Being gentle is more powerful than being hard.
It takes only a second to react,
but years to cultivate calmness.
Don't underestimate a calm person
it takes true mastery to overcome aggressive
tendencies.
Anger destroys wisdom,
and impatience erodes intelligence.
The choice is yours.

True power often appears weak.
Winning can sometimes feel like losing.
Rest may seem like stepping back,
and emptiness like nothingness.
But it's in these lacks that we find abundance.
What seems absent is often present,
silently and fiercely, just beyond perception.

If there is a desire simply to be,
you will face challenges.
But if you desire to be someone else,
those challenges will come with additional
problems.
It's not desire itself that ruins people
it's the desire to become someone you are not
that truly harms.

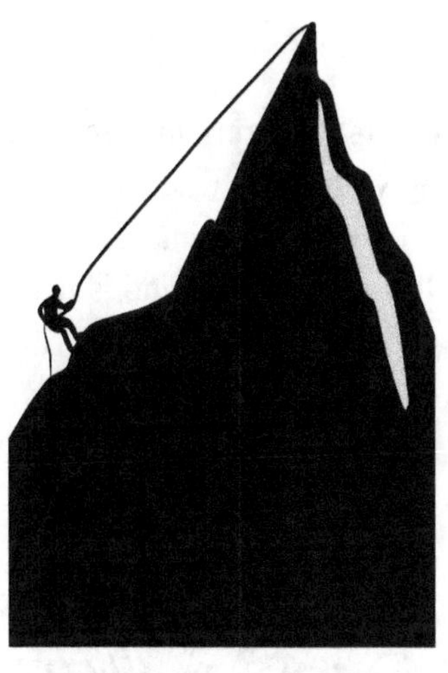

Work slowly and mysteriously,
with curiosity and determination.
Avoid showing off,
as it may lead to overconfidence.
If you wish to expand, first shrink yourself.
If you want to flourish, empty yourself.
To make peace with the future, don't battle with
the past.
Be present, and overcome hardship with your
inner gentleness.

Knowing others is merely information,
but knowing yourself is true strength.
Controlling others is domination,
but controlling your own mind is real power.
Everything you seek comes from within;
there is nothing outside that you need.
You must first make yourself whole.

Realize that you have enough,
and you will always experience abundance.
If you believe you need more, you will always
feel poor.
Accept misery, and it loses its power over you.
Embrace sadness, and it no longer haunts you.
Accept yourself as you are, what you have,
and everything that belongs to you.

Because there is so much misery in reality,
people seek to escape.
Seeing others with more makes them feel less.
It's not that you are truly suffering;
it's the desire to be like others that causes your
suffering.

A small mess is easy to clean,
and recent actions are easy to review.
Planning a day is simpler than planning a
lifetime.
Learn to handle easy tasks with great passion.
Do not rush, or you may falter.
To embark on a long journey,
you must take the first step.

Nothing in this world truly belongs to
individuals;
everyone merely imitates one another.
If you are being scolded, don't fret
it's just someone's opinion,
which is also influenced by others.
Don't feel overly pleased by praise;
it reflects the giver's perception and their
learning from others.
True wisdom lies in knowing yourself.
A truly wise person neither praises nor blames.
If you work for the well-being of others,
remain beyond both appreciation and
condemnation.
This will help you remain calm and centered.

Be a source of serenity for someone,
reassuring them that they are okay,
no matter who they are.
Avoid making people fall into the trap of
competition.
Appreciate them for who they are
and recognize that their social background
and economic status are beyond your control.
When listening to others,
refrain from questioning;
they already have their own questions.
Allow them to answer themselves.
This approach might lead to
the most meaningful conversations you ever
have.

www.ingramcontent.com/pod-product-compliance
Lightning Source LLC
LaVergne TN
LVHW011048200726
843509LV00011B/1367

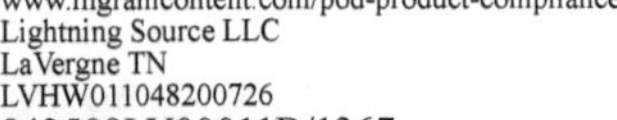